That's Wild!™

D1374167

Mighty Elephants

by Jenny Markert

®
sundance™
A Haights Cross Communications ® Company

Sundance/Newbridge Educational Publishing, LLC
One Beeman Road
P.O. Box 740
Northborough, MA 01532-0740
800-343-8204
www.sundancepub.com

Adapted from *Naturebooks,* published in 2001 by The Child's World®, Inc.
P.O. Box 326
Chanhassen, MN 55317-0326

Photo Credits: Front cover © Art Wolfe/Stone; p. 2 © Daniel J. Cox/
naturalexposures.com; p. 6 © Wendy Dennis/Dembinsky Photo Assoc.,
Inc.; pp. 9, 21 © Mary Ann McDonald/www.hoothollow.com; p. 10
© Anup Shah/Animals Animals; p. 13 © Stan Osolinski/Dembinsky
Photo Assoc., Inc.; p. 14 © John Callahan/Stone; p. 17 © Martin
Withers FRPS/Dembinsky Photo Assoc., Inc.; p. 18 © S. R. Maglione,
The National Audubon Society Collection/Photo Researchers; p. 22
© Joe McDonald/www.hoothollow.com; p. 25 © E. R. Degginger/
Color-Pic, Inc.; p. 26 © Mike Barlow/Dembinsky Photo Assoc., Inc.;
p. 29 © Mark J. Thomas/Dembinsky Photo Assoc., Inc.; back cover,
p. 30 © Renee Lynn/Stone

ISBN 978-0-7608-9343-2

Printed in China

Contents

1 Meet the Elephant!

On the plains of Africa, the afternoon is hot and quiet. The wind blows softly through the trees. All around, animals are grazing or resting. But lots of noise is coming from one spot. Large animals are splashing at the water hole. Some of them are taking a bath. What kind of animal is making all this noise?

It's an **elephant!**

This herd of elephants is bathing in a water hole in South Africa.

2 What Do Elephants Look Like?

Elephants have thick, gray skin and a tiny tail. They are the **biggest animals** that live on land. Adult elephants can grow taller than a school bus. They can also weigh more than 60 adult people.

Elephants have very strong legs. Their legs look a lot like tree trunks. Each leg alone can hold up the whole elephant. But their legs are not much good for jumping. An elephant can't even **jump an inch!**

From close up, you can see how wrinkled an elephant's skin looks.

There are only two kinds of elephants—African elephants and Asian elephants. African elephants are the biggest. They can grow up to 13 feet tall. They can also weigh more than 12,000 pounds! African elephants have large, **floppy ears** that cover their neck and shoulders.

Asian elephants have much smaller ears. These elephants can be trained to help with hard work. They even let people ride them.

Asian elephants are also called Indian elephants. This one lives in Kanha, India.

Almost all elephants have two **tusks.** Only female Asian elephants have none. Tusks are really just long teeth that grow out of an elephant's mouth. Elephants use their tusks for fighting enemies. They also use them for ripping bark off trees.

One tusk is usually shorter than the other. The elephant uses this one more often, so it gets **worn down.** But some tusks grow very long. The longest one ever measured was more than 11 feet!

Notice how much shorter one tusk is than the other.

4 ▸ Do Elephants Live Alone?

Elephants live in **family groups.** A female rules each of these **herds.** The elephants in a herd are loving and caring. If one of them gets sick or hurt, the others try to care for it.

Elephants live a **nomadic** life. They are always moving from place to place. The elephants must keep moving to find food. An adult can eat up to 1,000 pounds of food each day! So a herd can't stay in one place. It would soon have nothing to eat.

This herd of African elephants is walking across the plains of South Africa.

5 ▶ What Do Elephants Eat?

Elephants are **herbivores.** This means they eat only plants. Elephants munch on tree bark, leaves, and roots. They also eat flowers and bushes. Elephants need a lot of food. So they **can't be too picky!** They grab food with their long trunk. Then they pull it into their mouth.

This elephant is using its trunk to pull bark off a tree. It chews the bark with its teeth.

6 What Is an Elephant's Trunk Like?

An elephant's trunk is made up of muscle. It is very strong and flexible. Its most important use is for smelling. In fact, elephants can smell people from two miles away! They even seem to be able to smell water under the ground.

Elephants grunt and snort through their trunks. This is how they talk. One might bang its trunk on the ground to warn the herd of danger. Elephants also use their trunk to scare away enemies. They raise it high above their head. Then they trumpet loudly!

This Asian elephant has curled its trunk backward.

Elephants use their trunk to pick up food. They also use it to **grab things.** The trunk of an African elephant has two special parts at the end of it. The parts **work like fingers.** The elephant uses them to pick up small objects. The trunk of an Asian elephant has only one of these "fingers."

Elephants also use their trunk for drinking. But they don't use it like a straw. First they suck some water into their trunk. Then they **spray the water** into their mouth.

This elephant's trunk is reaching for low grasses to eat.

Female elephants are called **cows.** They have only one baby at a time. A **calf** weighs about 200 pounds when it is born! For the first few years, the calf **stays very close** to its mother. It also drinks her milk. The calf watches its mother and the rest of the herd. It **learns from them** how to stay safe.

This baby African elephant is learning to eat grasses and shrubs.

Are we there yet? Are we there yet? . . .

Not many animals will **attack** a herd of elephants. Most will not even attack just one adult. But sometimes an enemy gets too close. Then the herd **circles around** the weak and young elephants. Once the enemy leaves, the elephants go back to eating and playing.

Lunch? Fat chance!

The large members of this herd are protecting the other elephants.

African elephants have another way of dealing with their enemies. They just stick out their **huge ears!** This makes the elephant look even bigger than it really is. The enemies get scared. So they go away hungry. They do not want to get squashed by an elephant!

Hey! You talking to ME?

This African elephant is flaring its ears to look larger.

9 Are Elephants in Danger?

The size of an elephant does not scare away every enemy. People have **killed so many** elephants that elephants are **endangered.** Both kinds of elephants are close to dying out.

Sadly, people kill elephants just so they can **take the tusks.** The **ivory** from tusks is used for making such things as jewelry and piano keys.

These elephants are safe from hunters. They live in a national park in Kenya.

Today, most people know that elephants need to be protected. Countries have put a stop to killing them for their ivory. But elephants still face another problem. People have moved into their **habitats,** or living areas. So the elephants have fewer places to live and raise their babies. Some countries have made **special parks** where it is safe for elephants. With more places like these, elephants can be around for thousands of years to come.

This female elephant and her calf are protected in Kenya.

Glossary

calf a baby elephant

cows female elephants

endangered in danger of dying out completely

habitats the areas in which an animal lives

herbivores animals that eat only plant foods and no meat

herds groups of animals that live together

ivory a hard substance that makes up an animal's tusks

nomadic moving from place to place rather than settling in one spot

tusks large teeth that grow out of an animal's mouth

Index